Snow White

and

The Seven Dwarves
of the Old Republic

BY

L. HENRY DOWELL

BLACK BOX THEATRE PUBLISHING

CAST

Snow White
The Magic Mirror
The Evil Queen
The Huntsman
Prince
The Seven Dwarves

In the script The Seven Dwarves are numbered #1 - #7. They have purposely NOT been named. At the beginning of the play the audience may be polled in order to name the Dwarves. The actors must then act their parts based on the names that the audience has selected for them. In past productions a list of possible names was chosen through the rehearsal process and printed in the program. Some of those names which were quite effective and funny were:

Stinky	Baby	Farmer	Rock Star
Clown	Nerdy	Doctor	Pirate
Salesman	Nose Picker	Hippie	Janitor
Itchy	Sport Enthusiast	Old	Artist
Shakespeare	Brainy	Chef	Detective
Cheerleader	Cowboy	Tourist	Warrior
Nervous	Hillbilly	Spy	Robot
Director	Gangster	Soldier	Ninja

These names are only suggestions. Feel free to discover other possibilities. The lines remain the same; it's the way they are played which provides the comedy in the Dwarves' scenes. It is advisable to have a selection of props and hats backstage that might be used in connection with the names that are picked by the audience. Casts should be discouraged, however, from improvising lines during the performance. If played by a talented cast, this show has proven to be one that audiences return to for multiple performances.

Above all, the roles in this play should be played with maximum Gusto! Theatre should always be fun!

The action of this play is continuous. When a scene ends on one part of the stage, the lights blackout, but immediately rise on another part of the stage. If your production requires time between scenes, scene change music may be used in addition to the suggested music styles in the play.

SNOW WHITE
AND
THE SEVEN DWARVES OF THE OLD REPUBLIC

<u>Scene:</u>   The pre-show lights illuminate the stage. On stage right there is a castle wall with a large mirror hanging from it. The back of the stage contains a forest, and on stage left a small cottage of THE DWARVES with a table and several small chairs. THE SEVEN DWARVES enter and the audience chooses seven names for THEM from a list. This process can be handled by a cast member, or Director. Throughout the play THEY will play THEIR characters based on those names. When THEY exit, the play begins. There is SPOOKY MUSIC. The LIGHTS rise on THE MAGIC MIRROR, whose face now appears in the mirror on the wall.

MIRROR

Good evening everyone. I am the Magic Mirror on the wall, and I'm here to tell you the story of Snow White and the Seven Dwarves. Now first let me assure you that word is pronounced "Dwarves" with a "v" and not "Dwarfs" with an "f" as you may have seen elsewhere.

(Clears throat, comically.)

One snowy night in a castle far, far away, a little princess was born.

(A loud, crying baby is heard.)

Her parents named her Snow White. As the years passed, the child grew up to be a lovely young woman. Her beauty and her gentle nature won the hearts of all who knew her. But of all her attributes, the greatest was her lovely singing voice.

SNOW WHITE enters in potato sack,
singing a Motown tune.

MIRROR
You go girlfriend.

SNOW WHITE
Thank you very much.

MIRROR
No. I mean you go…offstage now.

SNOW WHITE
Oh.

SHE exits.

MIRROR
After Snow White's father died, she lived in the castle with
her stepmother, the Evil Queen.

QUEEN enters, dressed in black, and strikes
a pose.

MIRROR
As you can see, the Queen was very beautiful, but she was
also cold and heartless.

QUEEN
I heard that!

MIRROR
It's true. The mirror doesn't lie. She was also extremely
jealous of Snow White's beauty.

QUEEN
I am not!

MIRROR
Are too!

QUEEN

Am not!

MIRROR

Are too!

QUEEN

Am not!

MIRROR

She was also a little childish.

QUEEN

Just get on with it!

MIRROR

Very well…the Queen dressed the Princess in rags and forced her to clean the entire castle like a maid.

SNOW WHITE enters dressed in a potato sack. SHE carries a bucket and wears rubber gloves. SHE scrubs the floor. SHE works hard and sings "Swing Low, Sweet Chariot"

QUEEN

You missed a spot.

MIRROR

Despite the back breaking work and rough treatment, Snow White never lost her sunny disposition.

SNOW WHITE

I did miss a spot! How nice of you to point that out Evil Stepmother.

SHE exits.

MIRROR

The Queen's most prized possession was her gorgeous, antique magic mirror…let me tell you, it was beautiful, with a hand carved frame and a…

QUEEN

Ok, ok, we get it.

MIRROR

Every day the Queen would stand in front of her mirror…well, in front of me, and ask a question…

QUEEN

Magic Mirror on the wall, who's the fairest one of all?

MIRROR

And every day, the mirror, who was very articulate, would reply…

"You O' Queen are the fairest in the land."

QUEEN
(To audience.)
Darn tootin!

SHE exits.

MIRROR

While the Queen spent the majority of her time admiring herself, poor little Snow White had to work long hours in the castle, often singing and dancing while she worked.

DANCE MUSIC begins. SNOW WHITE enters, dancing with a broom. SHE exits and re-enters with a feather duster. SHE exits then re-enters with a toilet plunger. MUSIC ends.

MIRROR
One day, while Snow White was…plunging the toilet, she
made a special wish.

SNOW WHITE
Oh how I wish with all my heart that a handsome Prince
would come along and carry me away!

MIRROR
No sooner had Snow White uttered those words than a
handsome "Prince" appeared!

> PRINCE MUSIC. A purple light illuminates
> PRINCE. HE wears all purple with high
> heels. HE dances as the MUSIC blares. HE
> dances around HER. MUSIC ends.

PRINCE
Hey Baby.

SNOW WHITE
Why, hello there.

PRINCE
You sure are pretty. I dig tall chicks.

SNOW WHITE
Thank you…uh….Prince.

MIRROR
Although Prince was an interesting character, Snow White
was very shy.

SNOW WHITE
I'm very shy.

PRINCE
I can dig that.

SNOW WHITE
Have we met before?

PRINCE
I don't think so.

SNOW WHITE
You seem very familiar to me.

PRINCE
Of course I do. I'm Prince, and I brought you a present.

SNOW WHITE
A present! What is it?

PRINCE
Well, a present is a gift you give to someone, but that really isn't important right now. Here.

Hands HER a box. SHE opens it.

SNOW WHITE
Wow….it's a…purple hat.

PRINCE
It's not just a hat. It's a raspberry beret. The kind you find in a second hand store.

SNOW WHITE
Wow. Thanks big spender. I'll treasure it always.
		(Throws it into audience.)

MIRROR
Prince was quite smitten with Snow White.

PRINCE
I am quite smitten with you.

MIRROR
Snow White on the other hand wanted to take things a little slower.

SHE starts to say something, but then runs away.

PRINCE
(To audience.)
I love it when they play hard to get.

HE exits.

MIRROR
That evening, as usual, the Evil Queen stood before her Magic Mirror…

QUEEN enters.

QUEEN
Magic Mirror on the wall, who's the fairest one of all?

MIRROR
Well Queen, you see…

QUEEN
Mirror?

MIRROR
It's kind of like this…

QUEEN
Tell me!

MIRROR
Are you sure you really want to know?

QUEEN
Of course I do. Why would I have asked you unless I wanted
to know?

MIRROR
You may not like the answer O' Queen!

QUEEN
Really?

MIRROR
Well…

QUEEN
(Extremely mad. Yelling.)
Tell me! I command you!

MIRROR
As you wish.
(Clears throat.)
"Her lips blood red. Her hair like night. Her skin like snow.
Her name…Snow White!"

QUEEN
(Flipping her lid.)
SAY WHAT??? How can this be? She's so…cheerful and…
(Looks for another word, but can't think of one.)
Cheerful! Mirror, do you really think she's more beautiful
than me?

MIRROR
I calls 'em like I sees 'em.

QUEEN stomps back and forth.

MIRROR
The Evil Queen was so furious she immediately called for
her Huntsman.

QUEEN
(Screaming.)
HUNTSMAN!!!!!!!!!

> HUNTSMAN enters running. HE is a timid
> man dressed in grey and green. HE wears a
> green helmet.

HUNTSMAN
Yes my Queen?

QUEEN
Huntsman. Tomorrow I want you to lead Snow White deep
into the Black Forest and kill her!

HUNTSMAN
But why my Queen? She is only a child!

QUEEN
You will do as I command Huntsman, or I will have you
thrown into the deepest, darkest pit I can find, and you will
stay there for the rest of your miserable existence! Do you
understand me, Huntsman?

HUNTSMAN
Yes my Queen. I understand.

> QUEEN exits. THE HUNTSMAN lingers,
> uneasy, then exits.

MIRROR
Early the next morning, as he had been instructed to do, the
Huntsman took Snow White deep into the Black Forest,
where he intended to kill her.

The LIGHTS are low and spooky. SNOW
WHITE enters through the forest. SHE is
wearing HER Princess costume. THE
HUNTSMAN enters behind HER.

SNOW WHITE

Huntsman. Why have you brought me so deep into the Black
Forest?

HUNTSMAN

Your evil stepmother…the Queen, thought you might…well,
she thought some fresh air might do you well Princess.

SNOW WHITE

But it's so dark here in the forest…I can hardly see my hand
in front of my face.
　　　(SHE turns away from the HUNTSMAN.)

MIRROR

The Huntsman knew that if he was going to do it, it would
have to be now. He drew his sword.

THE HUNTSMAN draws HIS sword.
SNOW WHITE doesn't notice, though the
audience will. SHE kneels down and HE
raises HIS sword to strike. SHE turns and
sees HIM, and is terrified. BOTH freeze.

MIRROR

But he couldn't do it.

HUNTSMAN drops HIS sword and falls to
HIS knees.

HUNTSMAN

Please forgive me Princess. The Queen…your Stepmother is horribly jealous of you. She…ordered me to bring you deep into this forest and to…kill you…but I couldn't do it. I could never harm you. I knew your father…he was a very good man…and my friend. But listen to me, you are not safe. You must run even deeper into the forest! Run until you can run no more! And you must never return! Do you understand me Princess?

SNOW WHITE

Yes, I think so.

HUNTSMAN

Run then. I'll tell the Queen the job has been done.

SHE starts off, and then turns to HIM.

SNOW WHITE

Thank you, Huntsman. You really are a good man.

SHE exits running.

HUNTSMAN

If the Queen learns of what I have done, I will really be a dead man.

LIGHTS fade on HUNTSMAN.

MIRROR

Snow White was so frightened by what the Huntsman had said that she ran over the hills and across the green until at last she came to a small cottage nestled among the trees.

LIGHTS rise on Dwarf house. SNOW WHITE enters.

SNOW WHITE
What a charming little house. I wonder if anyone's at home.

SHE walks through door.

SNOW WHITE
Hello? Is anyone there? My goodness, this place is an awful
mess. And everything is so short. I wonder if this house
belongs to children.
(A thought occurs to HER.)
Maybe if I tidy up this house a bit, the children who live here
will let me stay for a while.

DANCE MUSIC. SNOW WHITE cleans
again. SHE enters with broom, dancing and
singing. SHE sweeps, then exits. SHE re-
enters with feather duster. SHE dusts, then
exits. SHE re- enters with floor buffer, or if
that isn't available, the plunger again.
MUSIC ends.

SNOW WHITE
(Yawning.)
Gosh. All this house cleaning has made me very tired.
(Pokes HER head in other room.)
Ahhh, how cute. Seven little beds. Maybe whoever lives here
won't mind if I take a little nap.

SHE exits with floor buffer. WORK
MUSIC. THE SEVEN DWARVES enter,
ALL wearing brown hooded robes, doing a
little dance step together and singing. THEY
stop outside the cottage, and simultaneously
each one does something to indicate what
THEIR names are. Then, THEY enter
cottage. THEY are muttering and
grumbling, and then all stop at the exact
same time and look around.

DWARF #1
Great Oogly moogly!

DWARF #2
Someone's been here!

DWARF #3
Someone's cleaned the place up!

DWARF #4
Who would dare?

DWARF #5
Look at them dishes! They're clean!

DWARF #6
Someone did the dishes too?

DWARF #6 exits to other room.

DWARF #7
Unbelievable!

DWARF #1
My fellow Dwarves…I believe what we have here is one of
them ghosts!

DWARF #2
A ghost that does dishes?

DWARF #3
I didn't know ghosts did dishes!

DWARF#4
How can you be so sure?

18

DWARF #1
Well, I know it wasn't the fuzzy forest creatures running around out there!

DWARF #5
Well of course not. That would be silly.

DWARF #6
(From other room.)
Oh my gosh!

DWARF #7
What is it?

DWARF #6
Someone cleaned the toilet!

ALL DWARVES rush into other room. A toilet is heard flushing.

DWARVES
(Offstage.)
Oooooooooooooooo!

DWARF #7
(Offstage.)
Who would stoop so low?

DWARF #1
(Offstage.)
Maybe it was that girl sleeping in our bed over there.

There is a beat.

DWARVES
GIRL!!!!

DWARVES come running back on in a
panic screaming and running into EACH
OTHER. SNOW WHITE enters.

SNOW WHITE
Wait a minute! What's wrong?

DWARVES stop. Beat.

DWARF #2
It's a girl! Run!!!

DWARVES run around again.

SNOW WHITE
Wait a minute! Wait a minute! Why are you so afraid of a
girl?

DWARF #3
Because girl's have cooties!

DWARVES run around again screaming
"Cooties!"

SNOW WHITE
Stop running around and screaming! I can assure you that
girls do not have cooties! I do not have cooties!

DWARVES have settled down. Slowly
THEY approach HER.

DWARF #4
Are you sure you don't have cooties?

SNOW WHITE
Certainly not. My name is Snow White. What are your
names?

20

DWARF #1

My name is __________.

> HE uses the name the audience has given
> HIM, and acts out whatever it implies. Each
> DWARF steps forward and does the same
> thing in turn.

SNOW WHITE

Those are very…creative names.

DWARF #1

Don't blame us, we didn't pick 'em.
> (Points to audience.)

SNOW WHITE

And do you midgets live here all alone?

> DWARVES look at each other.

DWARF #2

Excuse me?

DWARF #3

I'm sorry. Did she just call us midgets?

DWARF #4

I think she did!

DWARF #5

The nerve!

DWARF #6

We are not midgets!

DWARF #7

We're Dwarves! Don't you know the difference?

SNOW WHITE
Why no…what is the difference?

DWARF #7
Uh…well, we Dwarves…we're better dancers!

DWARVES
Yeah!

CLASSICAL TYPE MUSIC plays and
THEY dance.

SNOW WHITE
Gee. I never knew that about Dwarves.

DWARF #1
I'm sure there's a lot you don't know about Dwarves. And by
the way, what are you doing in our house?

DWARVES
Yeah! Tell us! What's going on? What are you doing here?
Etc!
(NOTE: The same DWARF should say "Etc."
each time.)

SNOW WHITE
(Beginning to cry.)
Oh…it's so horrible!

DWARF #2
Ah…please don't cry Snow White…you'll make me cry.
(HE does.)

THEY ALL cry. Bawl actually.

DWARF #3
(Crying.)
Why are we all crying?

DWARF #4
(Crying.)
Because it's so darn sad!

SNOW WHITE
But you haven't even heard my story yet.

DWARF #5
(Crying.)
Tell us! Tell us!

THEY gather around HER. ALL blow
THEIR noses simultaneously.

SNOW WHITE
Well, my Stepmother is the Evil Queen.

DWARF #6
Ooooh, she's evil!

SNOW WHITE
Yes, we've established that already. Anyway, she tried to
have me killed, so I ran away.

DWARF #7
Where'd you run to?

THEY all look at HIM.

DWARF #1
Where do you think she ran away to nincompoop? She ran
here.

DWARF #7
Oh yeah. That makes sense.

DWARF #1

Listen, Snow White, if you want to, you can stay with us. We won't let anything happen to you, will we fellas?

DWARVES

You bet! No problem! Sure! Glad to help! Etc.

DWARF #1

We were all great warriors once. In the days of the Old Republic.

DWARVES strike warrior poses.

SNOW WHITE

Oh thank you so very much!

SHE kisses DWARF #1 on the head. The other DWARVES are dumbfounded.

DWARF #2

I hope she doesn't have cooties.

SNOW WHITE

I don't have cooties.

DWARF #1
(Lovey dovey.)
She doesn't have cooties.

DWARF #3

What?

DWARF #1

Nothing.

SNOW WHITE

If you are willing to let me stay here then I insist you let me earn my keep. I'll keep this place clean and I'll cook for you.

                DWARVES
Cook?

                DWARF #2
You mean real food? Like fried chicken?

                DWARF #3
And cornbread?

                DWARF #4
And taters? I love me some taters!

                DWARVES
Mmmm taters!

                SNOW WHITE
And jam cake? Do you like jam cake?

                DWARF #5
Ma'am…we adore jam cake.

                SNOW WHITE
Then it's settled. Tonight for supper we will have jam cake!

                The DWARVES do a little happy jam cake
                dance.

                SNOW WHITE
Now while I whip up the jam cake it'll give you guys just
enough time to wash up.

                DWARVES
                (To audience.)
WASH UP???

                BLACKOUT. Lights rise on MIRROR.
                QUEEN stands before HIM.

QUEEN

Ok. Let's try this again. Magic Mirror on the wall, who's the fairest one of all?

MIRROR

Uh oh!

QUEEN

Are we going to do this again?

MIRROR

Well, you see…

QUEEN

Just tell me already!

MIRROR

Very well.
        (Clears throat.)
"Over the river and across the green, Snow White's still fairer than you my Queen."

QUEEN

SAY WHAT???

MIRROR

You asked.

QUEEN

How can this be?
        (Yelling.)
HUNTSMAN!!!!!

HUNTSMAN enters.

HUNTSMAN

Yes, my Queen?

QUEEN
Huntsman. Do you remember that little job I asked you to take care of for me?

HUNTSMAN
(Being coy.)
Which job would that be my Queen?

QUEEN
You know. The one where I asked you to take Snow White deep into the Black Forest and kill her.

HUNTSMAN
Oh…that job.

QUEEN
Yes. That job! Did you do it or not?

HUNTSMAN
(Thinking.)
Yes.

QUEEN
Yes…which?

HUNTSMAN
Not.

QUEEN
Not…what?

HUNTSMAN
Not. You asked if I did it or not. The answer is not.

QUEEN
And why…not…may I ask?

HUNTSMAN
Well…

QUEEN
Never mind. I'm sure the answer would bore me anyway. Do you know the punishment for disobedience…or not?

HUNTSMAN
(Very scared.)
Not?

SHE raises HER hands in choking motion. HUNTSMAN grabs HIS throat as if HE were choking. HE falls to the ground. BLACKOUT. LIGHTS rise on DWARVES standing around a wash tub looking into it.

DWARF #1
It's so…clean…and bubbly.

DWARF #2
Who's gonna go first?

DWARF #3
Not me. I had my bath already!

DWARF #4
When was that?

DWARF #3
Last April.

DWARF #5
Somebody has to get in.

DWARF #6
Who's it gonna be?

                    DWARF #7
Not me!

                    DWARVES
Not me! Not me! Not me! Etc.

                    DWARF #1
I know. Let's all get in at the same time.

                    THEY all look at HIM.

                    DWARVES
SAY WHAT???

                    DWARF #1
It's the only fair thing to do.

                         ALL shrug, then step in. If the tub is big
                         enough, ALL sit down.

                    DWARF #1
Now see. This isn't so bad.

                    DWARF #2
Shouldn't we have taken our clothes off first?

                    DWARVES
Aaaaaaaaahhhh.

                    DWARF #3
Is this one of them whirlpool tubs I've heard so much about?

                    DWARF #4
I don't think so. Why do you ask?

                    DWARF #3
I was just wondering where all those bubbles were coming
from.

Beat. Then ALL DWARVES realize someone has farted.

DWARVES
Oooooooooooooohhhh!

THEY jump out of tub and run away. DWARF #6 stays in tub, looks at audience and just grins. BLACKOUT. LIGHTS rise on QUEEN.

QUEEN
You know, if you want something done right you have to do it yourself.

In this scene MIRROR keeps sticking HIS tongue out at QUEEN, but stops when SHE turns to look at HIM. SHE holds up a magic potion.

QUEEN
When I drink this magic potion it will transform me into a hideous old hag and Snow White will never be able to recognize me.

SHE drinks potion. LIGHTS go berserk. There is smoke. QUEEN puts on hag mask and hooded robe. SHE holds a sack.

QUEEN
And now…
            (She reaches in sack and pulls out an apple core.)
Ok…who ate my apple?

MIRROR has been chewing something but stops. SHE reaches into sack again.

QUEEN
Let's see what else we have in here.
			(Pulls out a kumquat.)
What's this?

MIRROR
That O' Queen, is a kumquat.

QUEEN
A kumquat? What's a kumquat?

MIRROR
A kumquat is a subtropical. pulpy, citrus fruit, used chiefly
for preserves.

QUEEN
Really? I never knew that. Well, it'll just have to do.

			SHE pours potion over it and waves HER
			hands as if casting a spell.

QUEEN
One bite of this poison…kumquat, and Snow White will
sleep forever! Bwah-ha-ha-ha-ha!

			BLACKOUT. LIGHTS rise on DWARVES
			and SNOW WHITE. THE DWARVES are
			in line to head off to work, each getting a
			kiss from SNOW WHITE and then exiting.
			DWARF #1 is last.

DWARF #1
Beware of strangers Snow White. There's no telling what the
Evil Queen will do if she finds out that you're still alive.

SNOW WHITE
Don't worry. I'll be careful.

DWARF #1
May the Dwarf be with you!

> DWARF #1 starts off, then comes back for a kiss. SNOW WHITE begins to work. There is a knock at the door.

SNOW WHITE
I wonder who that could be.

> SHE opens door. QUEEN is standing there, in disguise.

QUEEN
Are you here all alone girl?

SNOW WHITE
Why, yes. Who are you?

QUEEN
Just a little old lady happening by. Where are the other people who live here?

SNOW WHITE
They've gone to work for the day.

QUEEN
Excellent. Excellent.

> THE QUEEN walks right past SNOW WHITE into the cottage.

SNOW WHITE
I beg your pardon?

QUEEN
Never mind. And what are you doing this fine morning?

> SNOW WHITE

I was just about to bake a pie.

> QUEEN

A pie?
> (To audience.)

How fortuitous!

> SNOW WHITE
> (To audience.)

 Fortuitous?
> (To QUEEN.)

How so?

> QUEEN

Well, you see. I just happen to be carrying a basket full of yummy kumquats here and I was wondering if you would like to have some for your pie?

> SNOW WHITE

Kumquats? What are kumquats?

> QUEEN

Well, they're a subtropical, pulpy, citrus fruit, used chiefly for preserves, but they also make great pies my dear.

> SNOW WHITE

You know, I don't think I have ever had a kumquat pie before.

> QUEEN

And what's more, these are very special kumquats.

> SNOW WHITE

Really?

> QUEEN

Absolutely! You see, these are magic wishing kumquats!

SNOW WHITE
Really? Magic wishing kumquats?

QUEEN
Of course. Would I lie?

SNOW WHITE
I have no idea. I just met you.

QUEEN
Oh, I'm very honest. Take my word for it. Would you be
interested in making a special wish?

SNOW WHITE
Yes. Yes I would.

QUEEN
Here you go.

Hands SNOW WHITE a kumquat.

SNOW WHITE
It's a funny looking little thing isn't it?

QUEEN
Don't judge it by its outside appearance Snow White. You
never know what it might be like on the inside…don't forget
to make a wish.

SNOW WHITE closes HER eyes and makes
a wish.

QUEEN
Now take a bite.

SNOW WHITE
Ok.

SHE bites into it. There is a pause as SHE chews . Then SHE chews some more. Then SHE chews some more. QUEEN looks at HER watch and whispers to HERSELF…

QUEEN

Come on…I don't have all day.

SNOW WHITE

You know…this tastes kind of like…urk!

SHE falls to the floor.

QUEEN

Now my pretty little Princess, you will sleep forever! Bwah-ha-ha-ha-ha!

BLACKOUT. LIGHTS rise on MIRROR.

MIRROR

Snow White had fallen into a deep, deep sleep. A sleep so deep that only the kiss of her one true love could awaken her.

PRINCE MUSIC plays. PRINCE enters.

PRINCE

That's my cue baby.

MIRROR

Hello Prince.

PRINCE

What's shakin' baby?

MIRROR

Oh, not much thank goodness. I wouldn't want to get knocked off the wall.
(MIRROR laughs waaaaaay too long at HIS joke.)

PRINCE
Yes. Ha ha. That's a good one.

MIRROR
Thanks. So what brings you here?

PRINCE
I'm looking for that cute chick that used to work here….uh,
Snow White was her name I think.

MIRROR
Well, Prince. She's over the river and across the green, but
she's just been whammied by the Evil Queen.

PRINCE
Bummer.

MIRROR
Luckily, a kiss from her one true love can awaken her from
her eternal slumber!

PRINCE
Really? Oh baby! Bring on the smooches!

PRINCE takes a shot from HIS breath spray,
then practices smooching technique.

HUNTSMAN
(Entering.)
Unfortunately, he isn't her one true love.

MIRROR
Huntsman! How did you escape the deep, dark pit?

HUNTSMAN
It's a long story and we haven't much time.

MIRROR
What were you saying? Prince isn't Snow White's true love?

HUNTSMAN
Absolutely not!

PRINCE
How can you possibly know that?

HUNTSMAN whispers in PRINCE'S ear.
MIRROR struggles to overhear.

PRINCE
Oh…gross!!!!!

PRINCE spits and wipes tongue on arm.

MIRROR
Huntsman? Are you certain of this?

HUNTSMAN
I'm certain. I've known this family for many years. We must
find Snow White immediately.

MIRROR
If what you've just told us is true, it may already be too late!

BLACKOUT. LIGHTS rise on cottage.
THE DWARVES stand around SNOW
WHITE, who is laying on the table. There is
a pause.

DWARF #1
Is she dead?

DWARF #2
No. She seems to be in a deep sleep.

DWARF #3
Can we wake her up?

DWARF #4
No. I've tried everything I can think of.
(Tickles HER feet. No response.)

DWARF #5
(Picking up half eaten kumquat.)
What's this?

DWARF #6
It's a half eaten kumquat!

DWARF #7
Oh no! It's the old poison kumquat trick! I've seen it a million times!

DWARVES ALL agree.

DWARF #1
This is the work of the Evil Queen, I'll guarantee it!

HUNTSMAN
(Entering.)
You're right, but we might be able to save her still.

DWARF #1
Who are you?

HUNTSMAN
I'm the Huntsman, and this is Prince.

DWARF #2
Oh, we've heard of you.

HUNTSMAN
So, she's in a deep sleep?

DWARF #3
It seems that way.

HUNTSMAN
Then only one thing can awaken her. The kiss of her one true love.

DWARVES look at PRINCE.

PRINCE
Don't look at me. She's my sister.

DWARVES
SAY WHAT???

HUNTSMAN
It's true. Snow White had a brother who was raised by her Uncle in the Kingdoms to the North.

DWARF #4
All is lost then.

There is a pause.

DWARF #1
Maybe not.

DWARF #1 bends over HER and kisses HER gently. SHE stirs. Then puts HER arms around HIM and plants one on HIM. DWARVES cheer. Finally HE breaks free and SHE rises.

SNOW WHITE
What happened?

HUNTSMAN
The Evil Queen cast a spell over you Princess. Only the kiss of your one true love has awakened you.

SNOW WHITE looks at PRINCE. HE shakes HIS head no. EVERYONE points to DWARF #1. HE blushes.

SNOW WHITE
Well, I always did like older men.

DWARF #5
We're not going to let the Evil Queen get away with this are we?

SNOW WHITE
(Rising.)
Oh no. No more Miss Nice Princess. It's time for Snow White to Strike Back!

BLACKOUT. LIGHTS rise on MIRROR and QUEEN.

QUEEN
Magic Mirror on the wall, who's the fairest of them all?

MIRROR
"You gave it your all you wicked Queen, but Snow White is coming to kick you're…
(Tries to think of a rhyme, but can't.)
…butt!"

QUEEN
Snow White? How is that even possible?

SNOW WHITE
(Who has entered.)
Oh, it's possible Stepmother!

> QUEEN turns to find SNOW WHITE holding green bladed sword. SHE grabs a red bladed sword.

QUEEN
The Dwarves have taught you well Snow White.

SNOW WHITE
They have.

QUEEN
Is it a final showdown that you're looking for Princess?

SNOW WHITE
Darn tootin!

QUEEN
Then…so be it!

> ADVENTURE MUSIC. There is a massive battle between THE QUEEN and SNOW WHITE. At one point, SNOW WHITE even pretends that HER hand has been cut off. Finally, SNOW WHITE gains both swords and chases THE QUEEN offstage. THE QUEEN screams loudly. Beat.

MIRROR
And so, with the Evil Queen vanquished, and peace restored to the Kingdom, Prince went on to become a music superstar, winning numerous Grammies and finally changing his name to a weird unpronounceable symbol.
(PRINCE enters, blows audience a kiss.)
Snow White married her true love, ________, and ironically, they had seven children of their own.

MIRROR (Cont'd)
(SNOW WHITE and DWARF #1 enter holding
hands.)
No one in the Kingdom ever touched another kumquat as
long as they lived, and finally, there was a large celebration
in the castle in which everybody got down with their bad
selves.

CAST enters. FESTIVE MUSIC. The CAST
dances.

THE END

Thank you for purchasing and reading this play. If you enjoyed it, we'd appreciate a review on Amazon.com.

On the following pages you will find a selection of other plays from the Black Box Theatre Publishing Company catalog presented for you at no additional cost.

Enjoy!!!

www.blackboxtheatrepublishing.com

NOW AVAILABLE!!!

"Poop Happens!" in this family friendly cowboy comedy!

So, Who Was That Masked Guy Anyway? is the story of Ernie, the grandson of the original Masked Cowboy, a lawman who fought for truth, justice and the cowboy way in the old west. Now that Grandpa is getting on in years he's looking for someone to carry on for him. The only problem? Ernie doesn't know anything about being a cowboy. He's never seen a real cow, he's allergic to milk and to tell the truth he doesn't know one end of a horse from another...but beware, before it's all over, the poop is sure to hit the fans!

Cast Size: 21 Flexible M-F Roles Doubling Possible.

Royalties: $50.00 per performance.

Running Time: Approximately 90 minutes.

NOW AVAILABLE!!!

WANTED: SANTA CLAUS is the story of what happens when a group of department store moguls decide to replace Santa Claus with the shiny new "KRINGLE 3000", codenamed...ROBO-SANTA! Now it's up to Santa's elves to save the day! But Santa's in no shape to take on his stainless steel counterpart! He'll have to train for his big comeback. Enter Mickey, one of the toughest elves of all time! He'll get Santa ready for the big showdown! But it's going to mean reaching deep down inside to find "the eye of the reindeer"!

Cast Size 23 Flexible M-F Roles Doubling Possible.

Royalties: $50.00 per performance.

Running Time: Approximately 90 Minutes.

NOW AVAILABLE!!!

At the edge of the universe sits The Long John Cafe. A place where the average guy and the average "Super" guy can sit and have a cup of coffee and just be themselves...or, someone else if that's what they want. The cafe is populated by iconic figures of the 20th Century, including cowboys, hippies, super heroes and movie stars. They've come to celebrate the end of the old Century and the beginning of tomorrow! That is, if they make it through the night! It seems the evil Dr. McNastiman has other plans for our heroes. Like their total destruction!

Cast Size: 17 9M 8F.

Royalties: $50.00 per performance.

Running Time: Approximately 90 Minutes.

NOW AVAILABLE!!!

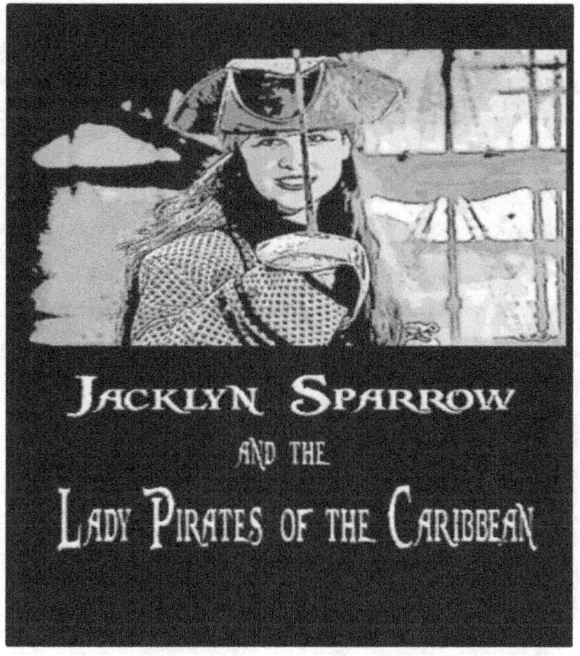

Jacklyn Sparrow and the Lady Pirates of the Caribbean is our brand new swashbuckling pirate parody complete with bloodthirsty buccaneers in massive sword clanking battle scenes!! A giant wise cracking parrot named Polly!! Crazy obsessions with eye liner!! And just who is Robert, the Dreaded Phylum Porifera!!!

Please Note: We offer large and small cast versions of this play. Cast and royalty numbers for both are below.

Cast Size: 45/13 Flexible M-F Roles Doubling Possible.

Royalties: $50.00 per performance.

Running Time: Approximately120/45 Minutes.

NOW AVAILABLE!!!

"May the Dwarf be with you in this wacky take on the classic fairy tale which will have audiences rolling in the floor with laughter!

What happens when you mix an articulate mirror, a conceited queen, a prince dressed in purple, seven little people with personality issues, a basket of kumquats and a little Star Wars for good measure?

Cast Size: 12 Flexible M-F Roles.

Royalty: $50.00 per performance.

Running Time: Approximately 45 Minutes.

NOW AVAILABLE!!!

"My dreams of thee flow softly.
They enter with tender rush.
The still soft sound which echoes,
When I lower the lid and flush."

They say that porcelain is the best antenna for creativity. At least that's what this cast of young people believe in Dear John: An ode to the potty! The action of this one act play takes place almost entirely behind the doors of five bathroom stalls. This short comedy is dedicated to all those term papers, funny pages and Charles Dickens' novels that have been read behind closed (stall) doors!

Cast Size: 10 5M 5F.

Royalties: $35.00 per performance.

Running Time: Approximately 15 Minutes.

NOW AVAILABLE!!!

Declassified after 40 years!

On December 21, 1970, an impromptu meeting took place between the King of Rock and Roll and the Leader of the Free World.

Elvis Meets Nixon (Operation Wiggle) is a short comedy which offers one possible (and ultimately ridiculous) explanation of what happened during that meeting.

Cast Size: 2 M with 1 Offstage F Voice.

Royalties: $35.00 per performance.

Running Time: Approximately 10 Minutes.

NOW AVAILABLE!!!

In the beginning, there was a man.
Then there was a woman.
And then there was this piece of fruit...
...and that's when everything went horribly wrong!
Even Adam is a short comedy exploring the relationship
between men and women right from day one.

Why doesn't he ever bring her flowers like he used to?
Why doesn't she laugh at his jokes anymore?
And just who is that guy in the red suit?
And how did she convince him to eat that fruit, anyway?

Cast Size: 3 2M-1F.

Royalties: $35.00 per performance.

Running Time: Approximately 10 Minutes.

NOW AVAILABLE!!!

Count Dracula is bored. He's pretty much sucked Transylvania dry, and he's looking for a new challenge. So it's off to New York, New York! The Big Apple! The town that never sleeps...that'll pose a challenge for sure. Dracula purchases The Carfax Theatre and decides to put on a big, flashy Broadway show!

Cast Size: 50 Flexible M/F roles with Doubling Possible.

Royalties: $50.00 per performance.

Running Time: Approximately 90 Minutes.

NOW AVAILABLE!!!

THE FOUR PRESIDENTS is an educational play which examines the lives and characters of four of the most colorful personalities to hold the office. George Washington, Abraham Lincoln, Theodore Roosevelt and Richard Nixon. Much of the dialogue comes from the Presidents' own words.

A perfect show for schools!

Cast Size: 10 Flexible M-F Roles with Doubling Possible.

Royalties: $50.00 per performance.

Running Time: Approximately 60 Minutes.

NOW AVAILABLE!!!

The lights rise on a beautiful sunset.
A mermaid is silhouetted against an ocean backdrop.
Hauntingly familiar music fills the air.
Then...the Lawyer shows up.
And that's when the fun really begins!

It's The Little Mermaid (More or Less.)

Cast Size: 30 Flexible M-F Roles with Doubling Possible.

Royalties: $50.00 per performance.

Running Time: Approximately 45 Minutes.

NOW AVAILABLE!!!

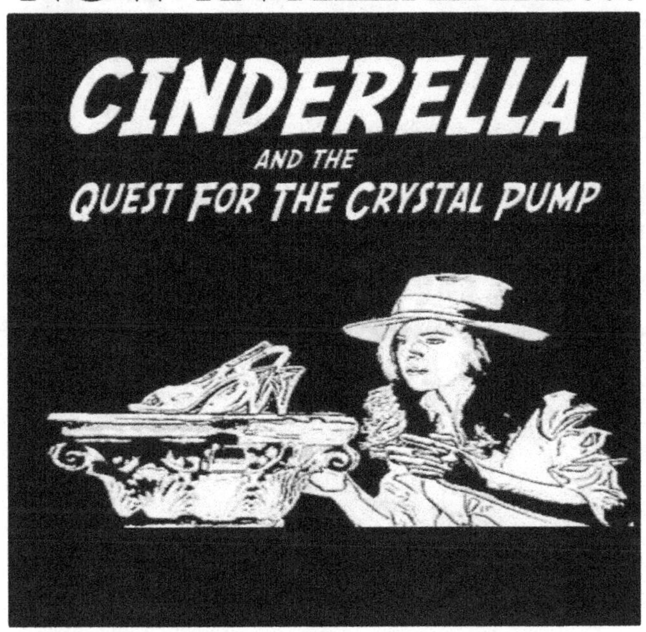

Cinderella and the Quest for the Crystal Pump, is the story of a young girl seeking a life beyond the endless chores heaped upon her by her grouchy stepmother and two stepsisters. But more than anything, Cinderella wants to go to the prince's masquerade ball, but there's one problem...she has nothing to wear! Luckily, her Fairy Godperson has a few ideas.

Please Note: This play is available in large and small cast versions. Both cast sizes and royalty rates are listed below.

Cast Size: 30/13 Flexible M-F Roles with Some Doubling Possible.

Royalties: $50.00 per performance.

Running Time: Approximately 90/45 Minutes.

NOW AVAILABLE!!!

Shorespeare is loosely based on a Midsummer Night's Dream. Shakespeare, with the help of Cupid, has landed at the Jersey Shore. Cupid inspires him to write a play about two New Jersey sweethearts, Cleo and Toni. Shakespeare is put off by their accent and way of talking, but decides to send the two teenagers on a course of true love. Toni and Cleo are determined to get married right after they graduate from high school, but in order to do so they must pass this course of true love that Cupid's pixies create and manipulate. As they travel along the boardwalk at the Jersey Shore, Cleo and Toni, meet a handful of historical figures disguised as the carnies. Confucius teaches Cleo the "Zen of Snoring", Charles Ponzi teaches them the importance of "White Lies", Leonardo Da Vinci shows them the "Art of Multitasking", and finally they meet Napolean who tries to help them to "Accept Shortcomings" of each other. After going through all these lessons, the sweethearts decide that marriage should wait, and Cupid is proud of Shakespeare who has finally reached out to the modern youth.

NOW AVAILABLE!!!

Everyone has heard the phrase, "it's the squeaky wheel that gets the oil," but how many people know the Back-story? The story begins in a kingdom far, far away over the rainbow – a kingdom called Spokend. This kingdom of wheels is a happy one for the gods have blessed the tiny hamlet with plentiful sunshine, water and most important –oil. Until a terrible drought starts to dry up all the oil supplies. What is to be done?

The powerful barons of industry and politicians decide to hold a meeting to decide how to solve the situation. Since Spokend is a democracy all the citizens come to the meeting but their voices are ignored – especially the voice of one of the poorer citizens of the community suffering from a squeak that can only be cured with oil, Spare Wheel and his wife Fifth Wheel. Despite Spare Wheel's desperate pleas for oil, he is ignored and sent home without any help or consideration.

Without oil, Spare Wheel's squeak becomes so bad he loses his job and his family starts to suffer when his sick leave and unemployment benefits run out. What is he to do? Spare Wheel and Fifth Wheel develop a scheme that uses the squeak to their advantage against the town magistrate Big Wheel who finally relents and gives over the oil. Thus, for years after in the town of Spokend citizens in need of help are told "It's the squeaky wheel that gets the oil."

NOW AVAILABLE!!!

Once upon a time, a beautiful princess was placed under a magic spell by an evil fairy. A spell that would cause her to fall into a deep, deep sleep. A sleep from which she would awaken 1000 years later.

It's "Sleeping Beauty meets Buck Rogers" in this play for young audiences.

Royalties: $50.00 per performance.

Cast Size: 13 with flexible extras.

Running Time: Approximately 45 minutes.

NOW AVAILABLE!!!

Santa Claus. Frosty. Rudolph. Jack Frost.

This Christmas…if you've got a problem and if you can find them then maybe you can hire…THE SLEIGH TEAM!!!

The team is hired by lowly clerk, Bob Crachit to help his boss, the miserly old Ebenezer Scrooge find a little "Christmas Spirit"!

Royalties: $50.00 per performance.

Cast Size: 6

Running Time: Approximately 45 minutes.

NOW AVAILABLE!!!

The Odd Princesses is a parody/mash-up that opens with a group of princesses assembled for a card game in the palace of the notoriously messy Snow White. Late to arrive to the party is the perpetually neat Cinderella who has run away from home after becoming fed up with being treated like a maid by her stepmother. With no where else to turn, the two total opposites decide to move in together! What could go wrong?

Royalties: $50.00 per performance.

Cast Size: 8 with extras possible.

Running Time: Approximately 45 minutes.

NOW AVAILABLE!!!

Eager to escape the clutches of the Big Bad Wolf once and for all, the Three Little Pigs build a time machine and travel back in time 150 million years to the Jurassic era where they quickly discover they have problems much bigger than the Big Bad Wolf. Much, much, much bigger!!!

Royalties $35.00 per performance.

Cast Size: 6+ extras with flexible M-F roles.

Running Time: Approximately 30 minutes.

NOW AVAILABLE!!!

Dr. Victor "Vickie" Frankenstein has just inherited his grandfather's castle in foggy Transylvania...but what secrets lie in the ultra-secret, sub-terrainian laboratory located beneath the castle??? It's a little bit monster story and a little bit Rock and Roll!

Royalties $50.00 per performance.

Cast Size: 16. 8 principle roles, 8+ Extras possible.

Running Time: Approximately one hour.

Made in the USA
Monee, IL
07 July 2026

56552162R00036